What You Should Know
Before You Commit to Dating, Marrying, or Starting a Family

To God Be All the Glory

By C. L. Ray, Jr.

PublishAmerica
Baltimore

© 2009 by C. L. Ray, Jr.
All rights reserved. No part of this book may be reproduced, stored in a retrieval system or transmitted in any form or by any means without the prior written permission of the publishers, except by a reviewer who may quote brief passages in a review to be printed in a newspaper, magazine or journal.

Second printing

PublishAmerica has allowed this work to remain exactly as the author intended, verbatim, without editorial input.

This publication contains the opinions and ideas of its author. Author intends to offer information of a general nature. Any reliance on the information herein is at the reader's own discretion.

The author and publisher specifically disclaim all responsibility for any liability, loss, or right, personal or otherwise, which is incurred as a consequence, directly or indirectly, of the use and application of any contents of this book. They further make no representations or warranties with respect to the accuracy or completeness of the contents of this work and specifically disclaim all warranties including without limitation any implied warranty of fitness for a particular purpose. Any recommendations are made without any guarantee on the part of the author or the publisher.

Softcover 9781615468188
PUBLISHED BY PUBLISHAMERICA, LLLP
www.publishamerica.com
Baltimore

Printed in the United States of America

Dedication

This book is dedicated to my deceased parents: Ollie F. Ray and Charles L. Ray, Sr.; to my sister, Hershel Lee, who passed away at the age of seventeen; my brother, Larry Wood, who passed away at the age of six years old; and finally my brother, Ricky Landoh, who passed away at the age of 25; and also to the late Dr. Noel C. Taylor Pastor emeritus.

Thanks Mom and Dad for believing in your children and thank God for letting you live to see three of us grow into men. You taught us to be the best we could be, to always find a way to get things done, and to never make excuses. We had true parents who instilled this motto in their children: Once a task has begun, never leave it until it is done; whether it be large or small, do it well or not at all.

Acknowledgments

I would like to recognize the following individuals who have made great contributions to my life and allowed me to return value to their lives:

My children's mother: Lolita Johns.

My sons, Charles L. Ray III and wife Heather; and Christopher Lafel.

My brother Danny and wife Sharon; my granddaughters Cara Ray and great grandchildren Nina McNeil, and Ania and AJ.

Special Friends: Dr Mark S. Churn, Pastor Emeritus of Total Life Christian Center. VA. Beach, VA, Pastor Churn is the most prolific, Bible based, word teaching and preaching leader that I have ever had as a personal spiritual mentor. Dr. R. L. Chubb, Humanitarian emeritus; Luther A. Brown, Sr.; Robert and Dianna Tucker; George Mccadden and Carolyn Abrams; Yvonne Dubose; Reverend Mary Billups; and Reverend Bertha Bennett. Pastor Lemuel Milliams, Faith Deliverance COGIC", Norfolk, VA. Ronald Bradshaw and Celestine Sparrow.

A very special thanks to Teresa Manalakos for her skills and ingenuity in design and layout, to Jenefier Winchell for her excellent communication talents; Janie Harrison for her financial acumen; Pastor Leroy Hill Jr., Reverend Raymond Dempsey, Bishop T. D. Jakes and Bishop Courtney McBath for their spiritual guidance; and Coaches Charles Price, Roland Malone and Harold Deane. Also, retired professor emeritus Lloyd Porter (Elizabeth City State University) and wife Josie and Lisa Wallace for her outstanding Business Acumen.

Contents

Preface *11*
Chapter 1: *Understanding Why You Are and Who You Are* *15*
Chapter 2: *Your Health Is Your Wealth* *22*
Chapter 3: *Use the Power Within You* *31*
Chapter 4: *Dating* *36*
Chapter 5: *Dreaming* *39*
Chapter 6: *Questions* *42*
Chapter 7: *Marriage* *44*
Chapter 8: *The Stages of Marriage* *49*
Chapter 9: *Cheating* *53*
Chapter 10: *Your Kids and Sex* *57*
Chapter 11: *The Family* *62*
Chapter 12: *Family Leadership* *64*
Chapter 13: *Why You Don't Own Your Home* *69*
Chapter 14: *Other Monetary Facts* *76*
Chapter 15: *Don't Depend on the Government* *79*
Finally *83*

What You Should Know
Before You Commit to Dating,
Marrying, or Starting a Family

Preface

The American Dictionary has several definitions of the word "secret". Here is the one chosen by the author for the purpose of this writing: A secret is something kept hidden, known only to one's self. This is so true and the information presented reflects how both genders can withhold their bad sides from each other, releasing only the good, and ultimately the truth will surface albeit after the fact.

Understanding education and its use through the revelation of secrets.

There is a misconception about education. Most everyone thinks education is power and that they're compensated in their chosen field because of their education in that field. The real truth is education is power only when it is effectively taught, understood and intelligently implemented and directed to induce others to reach a well-defined goal in a timely and effective manner. This is how and why one is compensated. The same is true with this information. Unless you read and understand it, effectively implement and direct it to add value to your own life and the lives of others, it will have no value to you.

The reader may think that some of the information that is presented first should be presented last, and that some of the information presented last should be presented first. In theory that may be true. However, the author feels the best way for the reader to understand the process of dating and marriage is to start right from the dating and/or marriage conception and childhood development. A tree is never planted from the top and grows downward. You will find some statements in this writing are purposefully repeated because of their importance.

During the lifetime of most individuals, they will be faced with several critical decisions pertaining to the information in this book, such as: *who am I, why am I who I am, what is my purpose on this earth, shall I date, if so how do I determine who I date, shall I marry, if so, how do I determine who I marry, shall I start a family, etc.* These questions are not all inclusive. These are not questions answered very easily, but hopefully the information in this book will assist you with some of the knowledge necessary to make the right decisions. As couples date, socialize, and hear and see successful dating and marriages, the successes serve as great incentives to date and marry.

Conversely, questions set in when couples see all of the divorces and sometimes abuse and violence in dating and marriage. It can potentially give them negative second thoughts. Couples face an awesome decision in making the right choice for a mate. Most couples are initially happily married. When a divorce, abusive or violent behavior takes place, the statement is then made that they seemed to be such happy couple, what happened. Human nature being, as it is, sometimes causes us to consciously or unconsciously hide the bad and release only the good. This is particularly true during the dating process. How to detect some of these hidden factors before the fact rather than after is addressed later in this book as part of a few secrets you may not know.

The unknown (although you can never know all there is to know about a person) is what causes the risk factor and has caused many a person to make the wrong decision. Every day of our lives we live with risk factors such as the unknown. From this point of view, you may make a mistake in choosing your mate. However, if you have made an intelligent decision based on due diligence and all of the information you have on hand at the time of the decision, then learn from it, grow from it and never make the same mistake again. Marriage and childbirth are the most risky of all the risks you may take during your lifetime. Finally, when true and lasting love exists, whether dating or marriage, there can be no mistake, only a labor of love. If you can have or acquire only a small percentage of true love as described in Chapter 5, your dating and marriage will be successful If the author can help the reader prevent a life-altering mistake, then the author' mission is accomplished.

Finally, you can prevent making the mistake of picking the wrong dating or marriage partner if you are patient, absorb and implement this information, and share it with your potential mate, or the mate you may presently have. The educational information in this book may reverse any present negative attitudes in an existing deteriorating marriage. Whether dating or married, each partner must understand that neither is perfect and that the mark of true love is the ability of each partner to recognize the weakness of the other, and become their strength in that area.

Chapter 1
Understanding Why You Are and Who You Are

You are who you are because of the following. First and foremost, you are a spiritual being. Next, your makeup consists of chemistry, genetics, emotion, education (or lack thereof), environment, thoughts, beliefs, attitudes, opinions, experiences, suggestions and parental molding. You don't control your chemistry, genetics, or gender. All of the others you can learn to control and set in motion. This can begin early on, during and throughout the ages of childhood development.

What happens when all of the above except gender, chemistry and genetics are negative?

In the author's opinion, it does not happen by chance or by fate. Of course there are unfortunate negative genetic occurrences that may happen during pregnancy and childbirth, which even the medical field cannot explain. It is my intent to only write about the circumstances which the two genders can control, such as discovering why they are who they are and applying the same principles to mold the child.

Use this education to successfully deal with the challenges that life presents. I repeat, the reader may think that some of this information should have been presented last and the last part first, however since the conception process comes first in our preparation for the miracle of childbirth and the beginning of the journey through life, the information is presented as is. As you read on you will see it all ties together.

Let's start from leading up to the planned conception, which should be one that is preplanned by each gender of the opposite sex. A preplanned conception should breed an extension of their love. A conception without love can produce emotional turmoil and a troubled child with many issues.

The husband and wife who are believers should be prayerfully concerned for the successful and healthy delivery of their child, asking God to grant them the continued love, patience, nurturing, understanding and successful handling of the challenges that parents will face. The husband should always be there for his loving wife, constantly reassuring her that all will be okay as he massages her abdomen, continually expressing his love and saying sincerely nice things to her. I must pause here and repeat that two of the greatest risks that are likely to be undertaken in life are Marriage and Childbirth. You can practically eliminate these risks if your marriage and/or conception is based on love, dedicated implementation of this education, and not lust.

Ladies first!

I think ladies are so special, so unique, and we men are so blessed to have them. We can't do without them and sometimes we can't do with them. They are so special in the eyes of God, for he chose them to be his premiere partner in the GREATEST

WHAT YOU SHOULD KNOW BEFORE YOU COMMIT TO DATING, MARRYING, OR STARTING A FAMILY

MIRACLE on earth: CHILDBIRTH. There are many loving successful mothers who did not become mothers by way of birthing a child, but rather by other means, and mainly because of the spiritual and motherly attributes they have been blessed with.

If you were blessed to be a preplanned child, or if you were blessed with on-going love from your parents, you more than likely received loving care; you had a fine responsible mother, and a father who bonded with you very well. The father usually has to work a little harder to bond with his children because the mother has the advantage of that automatic nine-month bond. Your dad should be your idol, always there for you; you can't wait to see him come home. There are many positive relationships with your dad. The word dad can also refer to step-dad.

Without you or he even knowing it, a worthy and educated father will be grooming you to be attracted to a dating mate with similar or greater attributes than those of your dad. It is automatic. You know no other way, especially between the ages of personality and character stage development, 4-12 years old, you may notice all the seemingly small things your dad does for your mom, like open the car door, see that she is comfortable in the home, and always showing affection. Later at the ages of 12-16, your parents must really begin putting emphasis on character and integrity. So whether you're dating or on your way to marriage, you now know what type of attributes you're looking for in the opposite gender.

When you miss all or a great portion of the above descriptions, you are likely to fall victim to the first sweet words that a guy whispers in your ear that you never heard from your dad, resulting in the selection of the wrong mate. You must always take the very best, worthy, positive education and apply it to any person, place or thing, and you should always be able to reasonably control it or the situation.

Warning! There are times when the female gender predominately sees all or many of the negative traits in the male gender that she is dating and likes the individual so much that she says to herself, "I can change him." Usually this occurs after they have been very intimately involved. Once that intimacy produces the desired feelings toward him, all the teachings temporarily or permanently go out the window. Just think of the many times you have heard a lady say, "I thought I could change him," or "I thought I could handle it." The real fact is, whatever behavior one consistently consciously or unconsciously exhibits for a period of thirty days or more will become a part of that individual. There are two possible ways for this behavior to be changed: 1) The individual desires to make a change, understands how the change will benefit him/her, and changes; 2) If the person is reasonable and you know and understand their highest value, you can change that person's behavior without the person even knowing it by appealing to that highest value. For example, you know that Mary places a high value on honesty. You catch her punching the time clock from work an hour early. You appeal to her highest value, honesty, and you say, "Mary, what you just did is not consistent with your highest value." This is an elementary example,

The deeper the negative behavior is ingrained in the individual, the more difficult it is and the longer it may take to bring about that change. Sometime a change is so deeply rooted it is impossible for that change to take place.

Men second...

Most of, if not all of the information under ladies first, is applicable to men and their mothers, fundamentally speaking. If the young boy has grown up under the same conditions, receiving love and affection, making every effort to be friendly with the opposite gender while at play and other child social events, it will be mostly because his mother and father have taught this to him. He will be polite to the opposite gender, respect and appreciate her, while understanding that each of their thinking will be different. It is not normal that two people will think alike. Anytime two people think exactly alike, if that were possible, one of them would be unnecessary. When men abuse or mistreat women, it usually stems from an overbearing, demanding mother or father. Where this behavior is prevalent throughout the male or female growth stage and beyond (if not corrected) and as the dating process continues, there are sometimes negative signs of behavior by both genders. Usually this is ignored on purpose and left unaddressed, perhaps for fear of loss of affections to some degree. However, when these traits are left unaddressed for whatever reason, they will always come back to haunt you.

Each gender can be great successful mates to each other throughout their marriage for a lifetime if they only apply the simple principals of Love, Joy, Peace, Harmony and Happiness, while respecting each other's values and be willing to give and take, and stop trying to impose one another's thinking on each other.

As the relationship continues to grow stronger, whether through dating or through marriage, the likelihood of continued success can only be maintained through the awareness of change in each other and the acknowledgement of that change by each partner. Time and change are probably the most important words in our vocabulary. The very creation of the universe and our existence is centered on time and change. There is no such thing as maintaining the status quo. We are either growing or moving forward or growing backwards; that is regression.

There are probably very few couples who do not observe and notice change. I think women are best at this, perhaps due to their great intuition. However, regardless of who notices the change, it need to be brought out front and discussed how to deal with it. Advanced dating, which includes longevity leading into marriage, certainly has its challenges and requires constant attention. Neither gender can, upon marriage, take the attitude, "Well, I have her/him now," and relax their attention to each other, back to change.

Three to five years into most marriages everything seems to be fine. After that, neither gender are likely to be the same person they originally married, because their personal needs have changed. If those needs are not fulfilled and the changes addressed, one or two things will occur: The couple will be miserable throughout their union or someone else will meet those needs and they will both have to move on with their lives.

A small example of change during the courtship and leading up to the marriage, and during the early stages of the marriage, usually 5-6 years for the most part, is that intimacy is performed at will and at the blink of an eye. A few years into the marriage and children arrive, then the intimacy has to be planned around the child or children. The husband hears statements like, "Leave me alone, not right now, I'm folding the clothes…" and the wife hears, "I'm tired, maybe later on…" These challenges are normal and can be adjusted; I simply mention them as small examples of change. So now that you know why you are, who you are and what reasonable characteristics you should look for in a person, the responsibility for making a mistake-free selection is yours. Please let both genders stay away from the thought, *I thought I could change him/her.* I warn you again if either gender permits themselves to yield to lust and become intimate before they make all or most of the discoveries listed above, their emotions will take over and none of this education will matter until after the fact. However, better late than never.

Chapter 2
Your Health Is Your Wealth

There are six types of health: Spiritual Health, Mental Health, Educational Health, Physical Health, Social Health and, Financial Health. These six areas of health have been mentioned in the respective order of occurrence. First, we are spiritual beings. Next, we begin mental, educational and physical development, followed by social and financial development. It is very important to be aware of these areas of your life and set goals in each area. When you set these goals and follow through with them, your life will not be boring.

Now let's address Spiritual. There are two types of spirits: good and evil. These spirits have been in our world since the beginning of creation, as in Cain and Able.

If you have been blessed with good spirits, GREAT. These are the spirits you will attract and will be attracted to. If you have evil spirits, you will attract and be attracted to those spirits. Evil spirits are self-destructive and counter-productive.

WHAT YOU SHOULD KNOW BEFORE YOU COMMIT TO DATING, MARRYING, OR STARTING A FAMILY

Mental: If you were blessed to be born without any birth defects (mainly mental) you have the mental capacity to learn effectively whatever you are taught and/or learn on your own.

Educational: From the moment you are born into this world, your education begins with the five senses. As a start, you cry and you learn that you get attention, you hear yourself cry, someone touches you, and you learn the sensation of feeling, perhaps without you even knowing that you're learning.

Physical: From your moment of birth, your limbs go in motion "a mile a minute." You eventually begin to reach, pull, kick and grab. You strengthen your muscles and ligaments without even realizing it. Educational health blended with physical health is very valuable, because when all is said and done, they may be the key to your longevity. Most of us have been taught to clean up the outside, which is very important, but what about your internal organs, the kidney, bladder, liver and colon? If you have ever had a colon cleanse, you know the importance of the cleanse and you may also agree with the author that it is a feeling better than sex. You actually almost feel weightless, like a feather gliding through the air. You almost never want to eat again, because you want to maintain that feeling. There are many books on this subject. Visit your local library, the internet or your local health food store. Good eating habits, nutrition and weight control are essential, right from birth, so teach good eating habits.

Social: Sooner, rather than later, you begin to mingle with other babies at home or daycare, and you learn to accept or reject others without you even misunderstanding it. From an adult point of view and in general, there will always be people that we feel uncomfortable around, for whatever reason, friends, relatives, neighbors, strangers, here are a few ways to consider how you may cope with such instances. Do not engage in subjects that your views are strongly different; refuse to argue. Always have the courage to respect the fact that both you and the other person have a right to their own opinion while never trying to force someone else to accept your opinion.

Always agree to disagree in harmony. Sex, religion and politics are subjects to prudently avoid. Never engage in an argument. Why? Because nobody wins, and there will always be hurt, misunderstandings, lost friendships and sometimes, outright violence. When someone tries to force an argument, ignore them. Ever seen a sane person arguing with themselves? An arguementive person is looking for a fight. Ever seen a sane person fighting themselves? In these cases the real winner is the person with the discipline to keep quiet or remove themselves from that environment.

Find subjects of similar mutual agreement and focus on them. When you get to know and reasonably understand a person, you are more likely to find areas of commonality and will discover more positive things about them. Everyone is different. No person, place or thing is all good, nor all bad. Look for and find the good in people. When you do this, the person is more apt to open up and let you in. This then becomes a win, win situation.

Consider staying out of a person's way. There are times when it is impossible to keep trying to be positive as you try to improve a relationship. When this is the case, there is only one positive answer. Respectfully and politely live separately as much as possible. This is particularly true when the other person is abusive or in any way engaged in unworthy activities.

The best way to live in harmony with such individuals is to love them at a distance, politely smiling when you pass them.

A clear agreement is very important, as stated earlier in this information. If you are sharing the same living quarters with someone, you need to have a very clear agreement regarding expected behavior and responsibilities. Once the parties involved understand this and agree to their own individual commitments, there is a strong possibility that you can live in harmony with people whose personalities you don't like.

You must establish what boundaries and behavior you will accept from each other. Put these subjects plainly in writing and each party need to sign off on them. While there are times when flexibility is an asset, you must define agreement-breaking behavior, for example loud and unruly behavior, too many guests in the house at one time, taking drugs in the home, etc. You may think that these suggestions are too time consuming and if you're intimate with someone, you fear losing their affections and friendship. The decision is up to the people involved. In a relationship of intimacy, there is a tendency for one partner or the other to yield to their feelings(weakness) and forego some or all of these suggestions. That is usually the one that ends up in Judge Judy's courtroom should the relationship go sour.

Financial

From a child development point of view you grow to a point that you see things that you want, and you learn that it takes money to buy things. You learn the value of money. The child must be taught the financial worth and moral method to acquire money and the financial value of things. Not much of anything we can do without money.

The last part of Ecclesiastes 10:19, states: ...*but money answers everything*. Of course this means within the scope of which money is used. For financial success you must always work from a sound realistic budget. Financially speaking and in general, there are only two reason anyone will do anything. 1) to gain a benefit; and 2) avoid a loss. Here is one way to do that. Take out a sheet of paper, draw a vertical line straight down the middle, on the left side, write "benefits to gain". On the right side write "losses to avoid".

List all reasons in both columns as you can think of. When you complete this, you will now have a basis for your decision, and it should be easy. One of the best ways to always balance your budget is to avoid this approach. See something you want with the mindset of I'm going to get it at all cost. Then there goes a potential financial blunder (the credit card) or bank overdrafts. Take the attitude of saving until you can pay for it. Lack of prudent financial control has caused the death of many marriages.

Personality and Character Stage Development

Personality and character development stages take place between the ages of 4-12. These are the ages that extreme emphasis must be put on all your child has learned and practiced. You must now implement a system for constantly

*WHAT YOU SHOULD KNOW BEFORE YOU COMMIT
TO DATING, MARRYING, OR STARTING A FAMILY*

teaching your child this information in a timely manner. When you implement this [information, you will be overcoming the major challenges that face all parents. When you make this a vital part of your teachings, look at what a relief you give our school teachers, law enforcement, our social outlets, and all areas of our society. This information will play a major role in your child becoming a good law-abiding citizen.

Between the ages of 12-16 the parent should be on the lookout for career molding, that is, noticing the child's interest or several interests and determining the strongest.

I can remember years ago I was consulting with a lady from Thailand named Zubadia and her husband, Tony, who was from Iran. They lived in Northern Virginia and ran a business. I had many occasions to be with them in their home setting. I admired how she molded the mind of her 12-year-old son named Sam. He wanted to be an architect. She would carry Sam out on the streets of Washington, DC on Saturday mornings, show him large buildings and say, "See Sam, one day this is what you'll be doing," as she pointed toward the skyscrapers. She further stated, "People from all over the world will be contacting you to design their skyscrapers."

This can be part of helping your child discover their purpose in life. It in my opinion that whatever the child's greatest worthy strength and talents are, it is a good indication of their purpose in life. (You will do well to well to help your child to read.) Here is how you can help the child discover their mission and purpose in life.

If parents or guardians have been blessed with only seventy percent of the information in this book, they can mold children in a very positive way and in so doing, save generations and generations from broken relations, broken marriages, violence, abuse, mistrust, unworthy evil thinking and actions. In this sense, parents control, for the most part, the road their children will travel. Anyone can stray at any time, because we're not perfect. However, I guarantee you if your children stray, the teaching of this information and for the believer, the Biblical teachings prior to their straying, will be so strong it will bring them back on course.

Read and research the subjects below. My mission is to add value to the lives of other people. I do this through the value of writings as it relates to their well being. You will be greatly rewarded to read all you can on the following subjects:

1. How to control the body
2. How to control the mind
3. Preparation for mental relaxation
4. Letting go of mental stress
5. Memory recall and visualization
6. Thought control
7. Study the spiritual laws of the universe
8. Understanding the importance of harmony
9. Your understanding of who you are and your connection to all things
10. Using your acumen
11. Concentrating on the truth
12. Understanding your needs, wants and desires

Some Causes of Failure

1. Negative hereditary background, such as brain deficiency (man cannot correct this)
2. No understanding of your mission and or purpose.
3. No ambition
4. Negative education
5. No self discipline
6. Negative childhood environment
7. Procrastination causes assassination of motivation, preventing idealization, visualization, materialization.
8. Compartmentalization and manifestation
9. Lack of persistence
10. Lacking in personality
11. Uncontrolled sexual urge
12. Always seeking something for nothing
13. Cannot make a decision and live with it
14. Wrong selection of marriage mate
15. Too cautious to take a chance
16. Close minded
17. Intemperance
18. Unwilling to cooperate with others
19. Unearned power
20. Chooses to be dishonest
21. Ego and vanity
22. Failure to acquire facts, rather guess
23. Under capitalized
24. Failure to have a detailed partnership agreement when living together, unmarried

25. Read the following books:

The Knowledge Book
Think and Grow Rich
The Road Less Traveled
The Man of Steel and Velvet
The Magic of Thinking Big
You Can Become the Person You Want to Be
How to Dress for Success
Books by Bishop T. D. Jakes
Books by Bishop Courtney McBath
Visit the Discover Life Bookstore & Café @
http://discoverlifebookstore.com
Visit *www.crcglobal.org*

Chapter 3
Use the Power Within You

There is a certain inherent power that I know the ladies have and for the most part, the intelligent lady will not use this power in an abusive manner. I have seen men become a great force of power; directing large organizations, speaking with respected authority and when they speak and demand certain actions from a subordinate, they can achieve any goal. Yet, the woman of his choice can weigh only 120 pounds and can take him by his nose (though he may be huge and robust), and still lead him in whatever direction she wishes. An intelligent lady will never let a man know this. When she does not let him know this fact and does not abuse her power, she will be more successful as she practices this control. There are the various types of powers. It is important that you know and test these powers before any serious and mature consideration for dating or marriage.

As stated before, if you are educated about a person, place or thing, you should be able to respectfully apply controlwithout abuse or chicanery. Here are the eight powers:

1. Title power: This is a power that gives you certain authority because of your title.
2. Reward power: This is power granted to you because of some reward or achievement.
3. Punish power: This is a power you have over someone who breaks a standard set of laws or rules.
4. Reverent power: This is a power of influence acquired from being well liked and respected by others.
5. Charismatic power: This is a power of grace, the divine influence on the receiver's heart and its reflection in his or her life.
6. Expertise power: This is the power that is evident when a person's knowledge of the topic enables him or her to influence decisions.
7. Situation power: This is a power which you exercise over a particular situation.
8. Information power: This is a power which one may have over the release of certain knowledge.

With the knowledge and effective use of these powers, you will understand that anything is negotiable and that everything you want out of life is either owned or controlled by someone else. Therefore, we are negotiating all the time. Now which of these powers do you and your partner posses? A great secret to using these powers in dating, marriage or any situation is to know the personality style of the person. There are six basic personality styles for the purpose of this writing. Most people will fall into one or more of these descriptions.

1. Analytical:

This type likes to get to the bottom of things. Curiosity is one of their strongest motives. They are known to be systematic and deliberately well organized. They like and appreciate information and facts delivered in a practical manner so it can be recognized as documented truth.

Their other traits are that at times they seem to be too cautious, excessively structured, and go by the book too much. They are conventional, orderly, controlled, logical, precise, systematic, diplomatic, cautious, deliberate, and disciplined.

2. The Driver

They like challenges and actually thrive on them. They are known to their peers as drivers. They are practical, very focused, and hell bent on getting results. They are to be commended for their ability to accomplish a very large task in a very short time period. This type personality usually talks very fast, are direct and to the point, and are very often viewed as direct, decisive and pragmatic. Additionally, they are action-orientated.

- Problem solvers
- Decisive
- Competitive
- Direct
- Assertive
- Demanding
- Risk taker
- Forceful
- Independent
- Very result oriented

Personality styles one and two are a broad example of the analytical personality styles. Most people will fall within these seven personality styles. The other types will be condensed.

3. Pragmatic style: Optimistic. Example: I don't think either side can win the military war.

4. Amiable style: They are dependable, loyal, easy going, like things that are friendly and none threatening, and don't like to deal with impersonal detail and absolute facts. They are usually quick to reach a decision, described as a warm person, very sensitive to the feelings of others, but also described as wishy-washy.

5. Expressive style: Enthusiastic, very out-going, high energy level, originators of great ideas, but usually do not possess the ability to see those ideas through to finalization. Really enjoy helping others, good at socializing, generally slow to reach a decision, can be manipulative, impulsive, a talker, and overly dramatic.

6. Extrovert style: This type loves to be social. Their interest is beyond themselves. They are not concerned about themselves, such as their own thoughts and feelings, often emotional, impulsive, and make decisions suddenly based on urge. They are very confident about themselves in a social setting and are involved in the lives of others.

If you have read to this point, understood what you read, and are willing to implement it and you are really interested in

*WHAT YOU SHOULD KNOW BEFORE YOU COMMIT
TO DATING, MARRYING, OR STARTING A FAMILY*

going slowly through your relationship(s) and into marriage and family. This means you most likely have not made a mistake. When one does not exercise patience and rushes into matters, they have primed themselves to make mistakes.

Chapter 4
Dating

Playing Married/Living Together

A great risk. Many couples take the risk using the excuse that, "I think we ought to kind of live together before marriage to see how we get along on a daily basis." This statement, of course, has a sexual convenience overtone. In theory, some people think this is not a bad idea. They use the statement, "Better to know what and who you're going to link up with for life." The fact is that once you find out most of what you want to know, there may not be any linking up, and after having given all they have to give to each other, someone goes away hurt. If you have read and understood the previous chapters to this point, you should be well armed and qualified to successfully find a compatible dating mate.

The biggest single mistake I see couples living together make is failing to have an agreement as to who owns what, who lent who how much, when it is due, etc. Then when the feelings wear off, the borrower (usually the male) tries to claim the loan was a gift. If you're going to play marriage, play by the rules; get the facts before the facts get you and get it in writing. A "live-in" agreement should be in writing, and it should include both partners' full legal names, health certificates, credit reports, telephone numbers of next of kin, legal names and addresses, how the rent or mortgage will be paid as well as utilities, the right to see each other's bank records (only if you have shared accounts), how expenses will be paid if either one is unable to pay their fair share, keep receipts as to who bought furniture and appliances, and how it will be split up in case the relationship goes sour. Do not lend each other money; direct them to the bank. You would do well to check your state's co-habitation laws. Playing marriage is also sometimes disguised as roommates.

If you fear the agreement will prevent your growth and intimacy, this is the best way to find out about the real integrity of your partner. If they balk about this agreement, then it's best to send your partner on his/her way. A word about marriage. I'm not an expert in this area, but to even the experienced, you must admit my advice is pretty good. However, whether you realize it or not, considering the above explanation on how marriage partners change, marriage can become a business, particularly where major assets are accumulated or one partner has a greater amount of assets than the other going into the marriage. If the assets of one partner are much greater than the other going into the marriage, then that partner may want to consider a prenuptial agreement. Some partners do not like prenuptials; they say it creates mistrust right from the start. However, the partner with the greater assets must chose between the thought of mistrust and the thought of giving away one half or more of his/her assets (should the marriage go sour) to someone who shed no blood, sweat or tears to accumulate the assets.

Chapter 5
Dreaming

 Everyone who has obtained the knowledge expressed in this book cannot afford to be lacking in visions and dreams. Without a vision and dreams, one is likely to perish. With visions and dreams, whatever the mind of man can conceive, believe, plan, schedule, and exercise patience, he can achieve. This is very important when you make your decision on a mate. Query your potential mate as to their dreams and goals. Be sure that each of your goals and dreams go far beyond just getting each other in the bed, for the beauty and the bed will someday fizzle away, then what will you hold on to? The true real answer is true love as described in Chapter 6.

 Now that you have the six areas of your life in order, it is time to dream. Whatever it is that you desire out of life, it can certainly be yours. For the believer, the Bible says that all things work for good for those who love the Lord. God works on our being from the inside out (from the heart); man works from the outside in. When one works from the outside in, they want to do whatever they want to, with whomever they want to, wherever they want to, whenever they want to, and as much as they want to, regardless of consequences—just do it. What good does all of this do if the consequences are fear, unhappiness, broken hearts, broken homes, broken relationships, and children in distress. What does this have to do with dreaming?

Here is the answer: Before you can expect the realization of a long-lasting dream to come true, your heart must be right. Let me clear up one thing here. A dream can come true without a pure heart of basic righteousness, but it will be of an ephemeral nature (short lived). Here is how to plant your dream. Planting a dream is similar to planting a garden. The farmer has a scientific dream. He knows that if he will plant the seed of his choice in fertile soil, that seed will yield its own kind, providing he will care for it by keeping the weeds and insects away while nature delivers the water to manifest its growth.

Your fertile soil is your subconscious mind, whether you know it or not. That is where your dreams are planted. It is better that you understand this fact, because then you can keep the weeds (negative friends, associates, family members, etc.) from destroying your dream while you nourish it with visual and verbal affirmations. You do this with the conscious mind. The subconscious mind is sort of a robot. It works 24 hours a day. It can do nothing on its own (except warn you of the potential danger and negative events) except carry out what your conscious mind plants into the sub-conscious mind. Before you sow any seed into your subconscious mind, analyze the harvest, the physical manifestation, and there you have the answer to your decision. The physical manifestation will be whatever you plant, good or evil.

Many times our subconscious mind warns us and when we go against its warning, the decision always comes back to haunt us. How many times were you faced with making a decision that you really wanted the answer to be yes, and a thought came from inside you saying "no?" You thought about it again and you heard the same "no." You overruled the no and went on to do as you wished, then when the situation back fired on you, the first thing you said after the fact is, my mind told me not to do that; I knew I should not have done that. Speaking to you was your subconscious mind or for the believer, the voice of God. I caution you, listen to it before making every decision.

Now finalizing how dreams work. A dream is first a thought. Thoughts, good or evil, cause action. The action is either good, worthy and productive, or bad and evil, evil is counter-productive and self-destructive. Pray for the success of your dream and ask God to bless it. Every lasting and worthy activity begins with a dream followed by idealization, visualization, and finally manifestation. However, the chief enemy of all of the above is procrastination, which can lead to the assassination of all goals and dreams.

Chapter 6
Questions

Get the answers to these questions before you date or marry:

Is religion important?
If so, do we both have the same religion?
If not, which religion will we agree to follow?
Do we both attend church regularly?
Do either or both have children?
If there are children, how well will either of us get along with them?
Are we worthy of each other? If so, why?
How do we know if we can refrain from lust and temptation?
Are we overanxious about introducing our young children(if any) to each other?
If so, we may be only interested in filling a man or woman of the household role and not a husband or wife.
Have we dated others for the very last time?
Have we informed our past dates of a new commitment?
What will each of us bring to the table? Is it equal?

Do we understand each other's needs?
Will fulfillment of those needs render each of us complete?
Do we realize that our needs will change as time goes by?
What do we not like about each other and how do we fix it?
What do we like about each other?
Do we want to talk about it now or wait for some disagreement and cough it up?
What are our family backgrounds?
What would we emulate from our parents' marriages?
How important is financial success to us?

These questions are not all-inclusive; however bringing them to each other's attention will reveal how much (or how little) you know about each other. As stated earlier, time and circumstances will bring about changes; however one thing will never change or vanish. That thing is called true love, which all receive from the greatest giver the world has ever known: God. (John 3:16)

As you continue your marriage journey, you will see each other's dirty laundry, but your true love for each other will still keep your marriage going strong, because LOVE bears all things, believes all things, hopes all things, ENDURES all things; LOVE NEVER ENDS. (1-Corinthians 13:4-7)

Chapter 7
Marriage

Please notice that the author has presented this information in a manner that will practically assure your completeness as to the six areas of your life as described in Chapter 2. Throughout this information, it is implicated that if you know better you will do better. In other words, if you are soundly educated about a positive behavioral subject, you will rarely ever behave in the opposite manner, because your education will tell and remind you that the particular negative behavior is self-destructive and counter-productive. Therefore, I wish every clergy, before he commits to marring a couple, would require them to read 1 Corinthians, chapter 7, The Living Bible, PARAPHRASED.

Men, I say to you right from the start, before you ever propose you should have your financial house in order. First and foremost, it is your responsibility to provide a comfortable and nice dwelling place for your special marriage partner. Be able to provide for her needs while planning for her wants and desires. Do not force your special lady in a marriage with constant financial stress. Be certain you are well prepared to

*WHAT YOU SHOULD KNOW BEFORE YOU COMMIT
TO DATING, MARRYING, OR STARTING A FAMILY*

give her a lifestyle equal to, or better than that style which she is reasonably accustom to.

Ladies justifiably seek true love, affections, understanding, financial and emotional security. Men, provide this along with sexual compatibility and you have a special lady for life. Men justifiably seek a caring, appreciative, affectionate lady who can be a loving, understanding, attentive, supportive partner and who can also make a house a home. This list is not all-inclusive, but it is a great key start.

To the special lady, I say prepare yourself to be a loving, understanding spouse, not putting financial pressure and stressful requirements on your husband that you know he cannot fulfill. Be prepared to make the dwelling place that your man has provided for you a home; only the mother can make a house a home.

The real deal, love or lust? This is a subject not willingly discussed by the average person. Why do people marry? Here are a few motives:

Parental pressure: Pressure from one partner or the other.

Selfish needs: Each partner marrying to meet their own selfish needs rather than truly meeting the needs of their spouse. These needs are not limited to, but include finance, emotion, sex, self-esteem and other considerations.

Unexpected pregnancy: Many couples marry from crisis pregnancy.

Just to leave home: In other words to get out of a bad home life.

Other cultures: in many other cultures of the world the bride is picked for the groom.

Although for the believer lust is a sin, it seemingly always follows attraction, dating, love or lust, then marriage. A potential partner may be attracted to the other through lust (I'm not indicating lust of sex). It could be lust of beauty or both; it could be lust of attraction, whatever that attraction is. If the attraction is successful in its longevity, both partners can learn to love and grow into marriage. What is love? I have heard many people jokingly define love as a misunderstanding between two fools. Of course, this is a funny joke. To the believer, love is very patient and kind, never jealous or envious, never boastful or proud, never haughty, selfish or rude, does not demand its own way, not irritable or touchy, does not hold grudges, hardly ever notices whenever others do it wrong, never glad about injustice, and rejoices whenever the truth wins out. By these biblical standards when you tell someone you love them, you may just be blowing smoke.

Love is loyal no matter what the cost, always believing in him/her, always expecting the best of him/her, and always standing your ground in defending him/her. Yes, love is the GREATEST. For more on this subject, read 1-Corinthians 13:4-7.

When you find that special person and you marry, the until death do us part, through health and sickness, and the whole marriage vow, is easier said than done. One thing that needs to be added to the vows, in my opinion, is this: Should this union produce children or if there are children from a previous union, we promise to faithfully communicate with each other regarding the welfare and support of these children until their legal adult age and never despitefully use these children to get back at each other.

WHAT YOU SHOULD KNOW BEFORE YOU COMMIT TO DATING, MARRYING, OR STARTING A FAMILY

Where there are children in the marriage, most every parent wants the best for their child. This is normal, however you must also realize that there will always be a lot of knowing, growing and teaching that must be on-going. For the believer, Isaiah 54:13 states: *All your children shall be taught by the lord* (this means through you) *and great shall be the peace of your children.*

Now on with marriage…for the newlyweds, don't believe what other people tell you about marriage, what to expect from the husband, or what to expect from the wife, or you should expect this or expect that. No two experiences are identical. It is wise to let each of you be your own true self, then be certain that you allow yourselves to love each other's true self, not each other's image.

At some point and time all marriages, like life itself, will become stressful. Knowing this, you both should commit and be sure to take the time and plan to do things you both enjoy Often, think of your pleasurable times spent together as a gold deposit in Fort Knox which each of you can recall and draw on during stressful times. Another good point to be realistic about is as time passes and you get used to each other you will need and appreciate occasional time alone.

This is normal. You may be one couple; however you are still two separate individuals. Both partners should be open to new and different experiences. Be quick to study and compromise to suggestions. This is essential, because for a marriage to survive it must evolve. We all are human and not infallible. Mistakes will be made, however when we show a pattern of understanding your spouse, if necessary, they will be more likely to confess any wrong doing. Should this occur, do not commit the cardinal sin, threaten divorce and use it as a manipulating tool, or become violent and abusive. Learn from mistakes and move ahead. Once a week, or certainly twice a month, you should do the romantic candlelight deal, give a romantic card often, or surprise her by cooking a meal every now and then, as well as taking her out to dinner. Surprise your spouse with nice reasonable gifts within the budget.

If you have read to this point and understood what you have read, I congratulate you. It is crystal clear that it is hard and dedicated work keeping a marriage intact by itself, but what about when the children come? The continuing education of your family with this information leaves absolutely no time for either spouse to be goofing off having affairs.

Chapter 8
The Stages of Marriage

Everything that grows goes through growth stages and marriage is no exception. Even the miracle of childbirth normally requires nine months as the conception evolves through stages. If you are newlyweds or newlyweds to be, or even already married for quite a few years, you are not likely to be familiar with the stages of marriage. For the most part, as young people, we think of life in a two-fold manner: pre marriage and post marriage. Through both thoughts you see yourself as married forever without any adjustable changes throughout the stages.

Nothing is further from the truth. A successful marriage means working at it. My objective here is to get the reader to see that marriage may be best understood when seen as a series of phases or stages that spouses go through while spending their lives together. These phases are interconnected, although separate. I call these marriage phases one through six. When you know these stages, you know that if you stay married long enough, sooner or later you will go through these stages consciously or unconsciously, It will be much better if you are conscious of these stages because then you know what to expect and you can plan more effectively as to how you can help each other whether the necessary changes and adjustments.

The Marriage Phases

1. The Honeymoon

Known as tender, romantic and one of the most thrilling times of the marriage. The honeymoon usually takes place right after the wedding and can last from weeks to months and in some cases, a year. This time period is usually characterized by sexual intimacy, passion, infatuation, marital bonding and extreme sensitivity.

2. The Adjustment Phase

The old adage, the honeymoon is over means just that. This second stage begins as stage one gradually ends for some couples and suddenly for others. This means that both spouses must be willing to commit toward the evolvement and longevity of a successful marriage. This is also a time when the preoccupation with each other starts to wind down or they get used to living with each other. The recall and realization of responsibilities includes work, family planning, in-laws, child rearing, and the list goes on as you drift back into the real world. Each of you realizes you are far from being perfect, while undesirable questions and behavior hidden during the courtship began to surface as you say to yourself, "Are these situations I vowed to live in for life? How did I get myself into this mess?"

3. The Three- to Five-Year Test

When the marriage has lasted three to five years sometimes an authoritative power struggle may arise. As the struggle continues, each spouse draws their boundaries and marks their territory as they seek to rediscover themselves in different and new ways that may preclude their spouse in some minor or major way. This may be overtly or subtle. Conflicts are likely to arise and may cause the need for marriage counselors. The danger of an affair may arise as conflict and frustration replaces the earlier passion and adjustments. Ways to minimize these negatives are discussed in earlier chapters.

4. The Re-evaluation Phase

When couples have made it well into the first ten years, they should become more and more accustomed to each other. Their habits, little screw-ups and aggravating things that irk each other should be more easily overlooked. The partners should realize they have now matured, especially where children are present. The couple should recommit themselves and become really dedicated. Rather than opting to bail out, they should review the strengths and weaknesses of their marriage and plan to enhance their lives for the better. It is very true that people let themselves fall in love and they let themselves fall out of love.

5. The Evolving Together Stage

At this point, usually the second or third decade, the couple has survived conflict, boring situations, temptations, etc., and makes a second attempt to rediscover themselves. The children are grown up and have gone off on their own. They should begin thinking of a silver anniversary, become very sensitive about their vows, and may have a remarriage enactment and another honeymoon.

6. The Mid-Life Crisis Phase

This phase can be alive and active in the female gender between the ages of forty to fifty years old, and sometimes as early as the thirties, requiring biological and emotional adjustments. This can affect the physical well-being of both sexes and suddenly they begin to see downhill, the other side of their married life. There is a sudden awareness of youth and a desire for a younger mate by trying to prove that they still have something that their spouse doesn't have—youth. Sometime this can cause one spouse to abandon the other for a younger deal—usually this deal is very ephemeral (short lived) and ends in disappointment.

7. Life-Changing Events Phase

There are many things that can affect the way each spouse views life now as to how they saw it during the marriage and honeymoon, such as a death in the family, unsuccessful, non law-abiding children, in-law problems, retirement, loss of job, sickness and a host of the unknown. These phases may not be a part of your union in their entirety, but you can rest assure that some of them will. We believers, including me, the author, are familiar with an old saying: "Trouble doesn't last always; there may be tears and weeping in the night, but joy comes in the morning." When you're troubled, read Psalm 46 and receive your comfort.

Chapter 9
Cheating

Why Do Spouses Cheat?

There are perhaps many reasons for cheating wrapped up into just two. First, spouses cheat in their relationship because they're having problems in the marriage that they do not know how to handle. (The information in this book can prevent these problems.) Something is obviously missing. Perhaps love and passion has diminished, they feel lonely, they find someone who treats them better, who is more affectionate than their present spouse. The grass always deceptively looks greener on the other side of the fence and in some cases, it may be. However, if you stay on the other side of that fence long enough; things will eventually resemble the other side of the fence from which you left. This is true because things are more similar than not.

Many spouses say they are just not happy in their marriage, and they seek love and affection elsewhere. I do not believe that spouses cheat due to a planned course of action, at least not the first time. I think that they find themselves in a situation where they're overwhelmed by chance, perhaps with a complete stranger or someone they know, and make a wrong decision of the moment. Recent studies show that from thirty to sixty percent of spouses have cheated at some point and time in their marriage.

Here is a rundown on who is most likely to cheat. Let me make this point clear first. When spouses find themselves in an ideal situation, they can be tempted to react in the reverse manner of their belief system. A spouse's attractiveness may indicate how likely they are to be influenced to cheat. Attraction attributes can be multiple in scopes, such as social skills, physical looks and money. The more popular one is the more her or she may be in demand, have a higher income, more education, successful career, too much free time. Those with separate social lives, career travelers, those who are by nature high risk takers, and those with high sex drives are the ones more likely to cheat. Research shows that two to three percent of all children are the result of infidelity.

Cheating, Telltale Signs

The dating or marriage agreement is like most other parts of our lives; your behavior establishes a historical pattern. Whenever that pattern is noticeably broken, it could be a preliminary sign of cheating. When the pattern is consistently broken, this could be a major sign of cheating. Human nature being what it is, whether dating or in a marriage, each partner wants to have a loyal agreement of true faith (except for early immature teenage dating).

*WHAT YOU SHOULD KNOW BEFORE YOU COMMIT
TO DATING, MARRYING, OR STARTING A FAMILY*

Once I was counseling a couple separately. The lady told me that her spouse was showing less affection towards her and the hours at which he came home had become progressively later. She further stated that when she begins questioning him, he states that he had been out with the guys. The next time it was that he had gotten behind on his work and couldn't leave until he caught up. After that excuse came the one that he'd stopped at a friend's house to watch them gamble. She asked, "Why didn't you call me?" He stated, "Well, I should have, but I didn't think to..." and the lies go on. Then when he did come home, he immediately hit the shower and unaffectionatly went to bed. As she made advances toward him, he shunned them off; he was always tired. This behavior could have very well been that of the wife.

Regardless of which spouse is showing this type behavior, if not corrected it is just a matter of time before one spouse drives the other someplace else to have their needs (whatever they are) met. Sometimes spouses will use the slightest excuse or justification for having an affair, and heading the list is an argument. One of the key telltale signs when the female gender is having an affair is when she starts consistently saying, with moderate hostility, "Don't touch me. I'm sleeping in the other room tonight," or when her spouse asks her to prepare a meal she says, "Fix it yourself." These telltale signs are not all-inclusive. A few more are listed below. You will do well to observe them. Here are a few other telltale cheating signs applicable to both men and women, and can help you determine what is going on.

You are not fertile, but you find birth control pills in the nightstand.

Close friends start acting uncomfortable around you.
The spouse stops confiding in you.
The spouse establishes a secret email account.
The spouse starts a body building program.
There is a secret cell phone account billed through their lover.
You find condoms and love notes in the car.
You start accusing each of affairs.
Your spouse is suddenly buying new sexy underwear.
They are no longer wearing a wedding ring.
There are marks or hickeys on their neck or back.
They abruptly stop having sex.

Chapter 10
Your Kids and Sex

When kids are about three years old, they're very inquisitive. How will you handle their questions? They want to know things like where babies come from. Will you tell them that a stork delivers the baby, or will you say mommies and daddies who love each other have babies? Normally, parents think of talking to their kids about sex perhaps when they enter middle school, just before their first date or leading up to the prom. That may be too late, because right from the beginning the child has been exploring sex all along.

Boy babies experience erections. At walking age you will catch them with their hands in their pants. When kids reach school age, they question what their body parts are for and what they do. In other words, they have been exploring while you've been thinking and wondering how you will explain the subject to them. There is a lot of difference in answering the questions of a three-year-old compared to answering those of a teenager. No matter how early you start talking to the child about the subject, you will do well to speak of the body parts by their correct name.

When a child refers to their private parts as their wee wee and they have to go pee pee, it can sort of give the impression that the parent is shy or ashamed to speak to the child using the proper name of the body parts. A parent should be proud to say penis or vagina, and say, "Do you have to urinate?" This type of teaching fulfills a two-fold purpose of vocabulary and the correct name of body parts. It also sets up excellent communications for future dialogue, and allows both the child and parent to feel comfortable in the conversation. Normally, the proper time for the elementary explanations regarding sexual boundaries, body parts and their names would be leading up to preschool.

Many preschoolers want to know why it feels so good when they touch their body parts and must be taught that this is not socially acceptable in public. Children vary in age relative to their sexual inquisitiveness just as in their maturity. Whenever speaking honestly and open to your child about sex in a manner of sensitivity, proper content, appropriate language and subject matter, answering only what the child asks, you can rest assure that your explanation will not be harmful. Like it or not, children will always engage in peer discussions about sex at some point and time. Since you are the bond with your child and in whom your child will (or should have) the most trust, faulty and misinformation from peers would be unacceptable to your child because you have told them the truth.

Young children are constantly learning about the world they live in and also about themselves. You should be a proud parent to know that your child is well informed on the subject.

*WHAT YOU SHOULD KNOW BEFORE YOU COMMIT
TO DATING, MARRYING, OR STARTING A FAMILY*

Sometimes children can ask questions on the sex subject that even the parent may fear the child is too young to know in detail. However, your child is better off learning the facts from their parents than a less reliable source.

A parent once told me that they gotten so carried away having sex themselves that they forgot the possibility existed that their young child might not be asleep and when she had an orgasmic fit. The child ran into the room and told her daddy to stop beating up her mother. How would you handle this? On another occasion in another situation, a parent got careless with condoms. The child found them under the mattress and was playing in the neighborhood blowing them up. How would you handle this?

If you want to understand if your young child has a grasp on your teachings about sex, you have the right to ask questions also. There is no better time for you to set the stage for your questions than during bath or shower time. You will always feel great showing interest in your child's sexual education and understanding as long as you do not force any issues on the subject all should be well. Parents should always ask their child how they feel about their body, including their emotions, their friends, and other things deemed relevant. Every parent and child is different, but it is the parents' responsibility to be open and honest, offering repeatedly to be available to answer any question at any time.

Well now, there are two sides to this story. So far you have been teaching and answering questions from the child. What happens when your child decides to direct personal questions to you about your sex life? Are you prepared to answer your child's questions? You had better be, and be truthful in doing so. If your child was born out of wedlock, or the father or mother left and abandoned the family at an early age, tell the truth. Don't wait until the child is of legal age and finds out the truth from someone else.

Some kids get a big kick out of asking their parents embarrassing questions. When your child asks you about your intimate experiences, it is absolutely none of their business and you have no obligation to tell them any details. If not careful, many parents will associate the sex talk with their children with the details of sexual intercourse. The subject of sex is much broader and complex than the details of the sex act itself.

Your children need to know that sex, as well as the activity, involves a number of aspects of a relationship, such as respect, intimacy, LOVE, trust and responsibility. Last, but not least, is Social Transmitted Diseases (STDs) The above descriptions cannot effectively be adhered to by the young and immature middle-schooler, high-schooler, or even young adults. The younger the age in which the sexual activity is engaged in, the greater the risk and the more it is seen as fun and games, sort of getting away with something for nothing. Then when an accidental pregnancy takes place and both parties are informed, the fun and games rapidly becomes dead serious business,

The children must be taught abstinence and that once an unplanned pregnancy does take place, neither his nor her life will ever be the same. For the young, immature, insecure and uneducated, it is the beginning of a financial nightmare. Of course you cannot be with them 24 hours a day; all you can do is educate, supervise as closely as possible, and let go.

Don't reconcile yourself to the idea that your children will have sex at a younger age regardless. According to a recent report by CDC, 50% of high school students have had sex and half of the students have not. Do you know what category your child is in? Although there are many factors that contribute to teenage sex, a study by a major teen magazine and the Kaiser Family Foundation indicated that more than nine out of ten teenagers agreed being a VIRGIN is a good thing.

The same study indicated that those maintaining abstinence recognized these benefits, respect from peers, and control and freedom from worry of pregnancy and STDs. So to the parents I say, by educating yourself first and then your children, you really can make a difference in the life of your child. This is done with honest and ongoing conversation on the consequences of sexual behavior, the risk of STDs, and the emotional and financial drama. This is paramount during the high school years.

Finally, talk is cheap. If you're wearing tight tights and twisting when you walk and showing all your cleavage, you may be sending confusing messages about sex to your child. Does your thong show? Do you use the wrong sexual language in your home or are you always speaking the wrong language about the opposite sex? Kids are masters when it comes to picking up cues between Mom and Dad, especially when it comes to sexuality. Whether it be a loving kiss or a full-blown argument between parents, it makes quite an impression on children. Peers have an insurmountable influence during the preteen and teenage years. However, parents still rule as the ultimate mentor. Seeing your sexual attitudes and habits through your child's eyes may provide an eye-opening perspective as well as a strong incentive to behave in a manner you want your child to model.

Chapter 11
The Family

The word "family" has several definitions. For the purpose of this writing, the following definition is used:

The family is a group of individuals with a continuing legal, genetic and/or emotional relationship. Society relies on the family group to provide for the economic and protective needs of individuals, especially children and the elderly in today's world. There are same genders creating a family unit, however this type family unit is not the norm. There are many successful, single-parent, incomplete families. These are called incomplete because one of the parents is missing for whatever reason.

The family unit is usually comprised of a recognized head of household authority figure whose main responsibility is to provide for the needs of the family and to see that the laws of the family system are not broken. The ideal head of household authority is usually the father where there are two parents. The mother is usually the caretaker and overseer of the family's internal structure and her main responsibility is being a mother to the children and assure that she makes the house a home.

WHAT YOU SHOULD KNOW BEFORE YOU COMMIT TO DATING, MARRYING, OR STARTING A FAMILY

The husband must have compassion with the wife, who may also be employed in the workplace.

It is a known fact that a woman's work is never done, and when she comes home from work, her job just begins. In this case, the husband cannot put the full internal workload on the wife. The family, when structured properly, can be referred to as a success system, mainly because of an established system that produces positive results. The family should be taught that the motto is "all for one and one for all". If you consider your family blessed, remember this: We must all give back something in return for what we have received. Plant a blessing into the life of someone with diabetes. Go to this URL: http://charlesray.g12.com/ and make your tax-deductible donation be sure to say you saw link in the Ray Book.

In conclusion of this brief statement about family, I will end it by saying that no one is perfect. There is no information on how to be the perfect parent or the perfect child. We all make mistakes in the family. Like life itself, there will be ups and downs, there will be tears of joy, tears of sadness, but all in all we are dealt a deck of cards to play the game of life, and we must play the hand we're dealt. If the information in this book has added value to your life and the lives of those you love and care about, then another part of my mission has been fulfilled.

Chapter 12
Family Leadership

Leadership, Expecting the Best

Everyone who has realized success, no matter what the endeavor, expected nothing short of excellence of himself/herself first, and nothing short of excellence in others second. If you desire to realize success, you must expect nothing short of excellence in yourself in your commitment to work your system according to your action plan in building your success.

Look at this as if it were your job, because it is. You will read that I repeat several phrases or sentences, because of their importance; as they relate to excellence; their value is worth repeating. Be your own employer and expect nothing short of excellence in yourself. Every morning look at yourself in the mirror and interview that person who is looking at you for the job that is today's activity. After four hours, go and stand in front of that mirror again and either congratulate that person looking at you and take him or her to lunch; or fire yourself.

If you've just fired yourself, then turn around and reapply

for the job again. How badly do you want success? How strong are your emotions? You, the employer, should expect nothing short of excellence from you, the employee. You are your own creation, no one else's. You are your own victim, not a victim of circumstances. Set your goals high and strive with all your might to meet them. You may not always meet your goal, but you will realize success. Has Martin Luther King's dream come to pass in its entirety? Definitely not, but he was tremendously successful in what has been realized.

When you follow every point that has been discussed on pages and are committed to following through with your activity plan and your method of operation day by day, week by week, month by month, you will build incredible success; success that you never thought possible. Read and study this information until it becomes a part of you.

Leadership Is Reacting Properly to Change

It is a fact that you will experience pain during your life! The question is, what type of pain will you experience as the consequences of your decisions and actions today? Are you choosing the pain of change, or will you experience the pain of regret later in life? The reward for choosing the pain of change today can be the realization of your dreams. The pain of regret only leads to depression and the loathing of yourself. Which pain will you experience, the pain of change or the pain of regret? Your actions right NOW determine which pain you will experience. Everyone who has succeeded in life has gone through the pain of change before realizing success.

Every day you are faced with choices. It was the decision you made concerning those choices that define who you are today. It is the decision you make right now that will determine what your tomorrow will be. You can say, "I can't," and not even try, or you can say, "I can and will," by acting right NOW to build your field of dreams. The measure of change is results.

Leadership Is Knowing That for All Actions There Are Reactions

I have stated this earlier in this book: everything you do and every decision you make in life has a consequence. Right now you are living proof of everything you have done and every decision you have ever made. Are you happy with your creation? If not, then you must diligently follow a corrective plan of action. Who is the fool the architect—or the builder who builds without a plan? By what method are you building your dream? Pretend that you have lived your entire life in Miami, Florida, without ever leaving. Would you enter an automobile race to Anchorage, Alaska, without taking a road map? Of course not! The chances of you crossing the United States and finding the one road that leads to Alaska though Canada with no idea in which direction Alaska lies would be next to impossible. How could you expect to win without a road map?

The above illustration holds true for your success in life as well. Take the road map provided for you in this information, pinpoint your destination and plot your course. The entire information in this book is a systematic blueprint for success in the total areas of your life. Success is not an accident that happened; it is the consequences of action within the boundaries of a proven system. Are you in action yet, or are you just reading? Reading and thinking about this system will do nothing for you financially. You must act NOW and do these exercises on paper. You must draw it out where you can visibly see it, and then share it with others whom you would not want to disappoint. When you follow this information, you will guarantee your success. All the good and prosperity that you wish for yourself, wish it for others your wish will then be more powerful and fulfilling.

Sometimes Real Leadership Involves Risk

You are living proof of all your actions so far. If you are not living your dream, it is because you are living in a rut of comfort. You must do something different if you want to realize your dream, or your dream will remain a dream until it dies as you lose hope. Understand one thing: your failure at achieving your dream is solely your doing. As long as you continue to blame something or someone other than yourself for your predicament, you will never live your dream. You must get out of your comfort zone, take action and face your fears. Do the exercises, set your goals, create your action plan, and work your system with passion, conviction, commitment, and most importantly, LOVE. When a soldier is in battle with his life on the line, he is in constant fear and will do whatever it takes to win the battle. Leaders have the same attitude toward achieving their dream. They go for broke, they put all their efforts on the line, get out there, and do what it takes to realize their goal and live their dream in reality. A success plan takes off like a train.

A train takes off slowly with the engines working at full capacity. You can hear a deafening roar thunder for miles, yet the train is barely moving. However, as the train gains momentum, the engines work less and less until at peak speed, the engines are nearly coasting with little effort being exerted to keep the train moving. The only sound heard when the train is cruising is the thunder created by its movement; the engines themselves are not heard. Your success system is the same way. You need to start off with a massive effort, but if you work your action plan, following your system for success, it will all have been worth it once your team is built and your train is cruising at sonic speed.

In conclusion of this brief statement about family (I repeat), I will end it by saying, no one is perfect. There is no information on how to be the perfect parent or the perfect child. We all make mistakes in the family, like life itself; there will be ups and downs. There will be tears of joy and tears of sadness. All in all we are dealt a deck of cards to play the game of life and we must play the hand we're dealt. If the information in this book has added value to your life and the lives of those you love and care about, then another part of my mission has been fulfilled.

The Financial System

Chapter 13
Why You Don't Own Your Home

Why you don't own your home, even if you have the deed marked paid in full...

The Federal Reserve.

You hear about it on TV, you read about it in the newspapers, you see the words written on every American dollar bill. Just WHAT is the Federal Reserve anyway? Most people think: 1) it's just another branch of the United States Government; 2) it has something to do with the United States Treasury Department; and/or 3) it has something to do with the printing of money. Well, if you thought it has something to do with the U. S. Department of the Treasury and that it has something to do with the printing of American money, you're correct. But if you thought it was just another branch of the United States Government, you're DEAD WRONG!

Here is an explanation. The "Federal Reserve" is not a branch of the United States Government! In fact, it has absolutely nothing to do with the U. S. Government-with one exception (which will be explained later). If you don't believe this, look under the government listings in the white pages of your telephone directory. You will not find the Federal Reserve listed. The Federal Reserve, also known as "The Fed", is a multi-trillion dollar PRIVATE CORPORATION! Few people know this. Even fewer know who the individuals are that actually own the Federal Reserve. The "individuals" are actually very wealthy FAMILIES, some of whose names you've heard before.

There are eight families alleged to own the Federal Reserve. They are:

1. The "Rothschilds" of Europe
2. The "Lizards" of Paris
3. The "Israel Moses Seifs" of Italy
4. The "Warburgs" of Germany
5. The "Lehmans" of New York
6. The "Kuhn-Loebs" of New York
7. The "Goldman-Sachs" of New York
8. The "Rockefellers" of New York

These eight families control your life…whether you are aware of it or not. Whether you believe it or not, it doesn't change the fact, these eight families pretty much control the lives of the ENTIRE world, because they control most of the MONEY in the entire world. To explain in detail gets quite complicated, so the discussion will be somewhat limited in this text to a "beefed" down, simplified, and (hopefully) understandable explanation. We'll limit our discussion as to how people in the U. S. are affected. This information is new to the vast majority of U. S. Citizens and there is not room here in this text to tell everything there is to know about The Federal Reserve, however for more information on this subject, you may visit your public Library.

Here's how the Federal Reserve Took Control of our money:

Rich international bankers have long sought to control the financial system of the United States of America, for they knew that whoever controlled the money also controlled the making of its laws. This fact dates back to the U.S.'s earliest beginning in the late 1700's. In Benjamin Franklin's autobiography, it is reported that he wrote, "The inability of the colonists to issue their own money permanently out of the hands of [king] George III and the international bankers was the prime reason for the Revolutionary War." Countless attempts were made throughout the 1800's and into the early 1900's to control the U. S. monetary system. Presidents Andrew Jackson, Abraham Lincoln, James Garfield and William McKinley all fiercely battled the rich international bankers. Despite the opposition, the bankers succeeded in controlling the U. S. monetary system on several "limited terms" throughout this period of time.

In 1913, the bankers finally were successful in achieving their aspirations. Thanks to the many dishonest politicians in office at the time, they were able to get "The Federal Reserve Act" passed through Congress. The bankers could now run the country on an "unlimited term" basis by controlling the creation of money in the U. S. This is in direct violation the constitution as written by the Founding Fathers. The constitution clearly states that only Congress shall have the power to coin and regulate money. With the establishment of the Federal Reserve Act in 1913, power was transferred to a rich group of bankers to coin and regulate money in the U. S.

How the Takeover Happened

Between 1914 and 1929, Congress spent four paper dollars for each one dollar's worth of gold and silver in the U. S. Treasury. The Great Depression of 1929 saw the Treasury with a "public debt" of about $17 billion in gold and silver owed to the Federal Reserve. By June of 1933, the end of the original twenty-year charter of the Federal Reserve, the Treasury was empty; all the gold and silver had been "pledged" as payment for the U. S. debt to the Federal Reserve. At this point, the Federal Reserve foreclosed on the U. S. Government's outstanding obligations, bringing about HJR (House Joint Resolution) 192 in Congress. HJR 192 suspended the gold standard and abrogated the gold clause. The U. S. Treasure was bankrupt on June 5, 1933. With the knowledge, consent and assistance of the criminal officials in Washington, DC, all the gold and silver that most citizens thought was in Fort Knox had been moved to the banks in Switzerland and the vaults of the Federal Reserve in New York. No longer were they in the possession of the United States Government.

Here is the reason for title of this chapter:

Within the next four years after the 1933 Bankruptcy, President Franklin Delano Roosevelt had by contract, unlawfully and criminally pledged all land in America to the Federal Reserve in exchange for "continued debt-credit support". "All Land" means your home, business, car, etc., anything you have that has ever had a mortgage or loan against it or was paid for with Federal Reserve Notes (money)

WHAT YOU SHOULD KNOW BEFORE YOU COMMIT TO DATING, MARRYING, OR STARTING A FAMILY

Understanding the Money System

The paper we "exchange" for goods and services is what we call "money". American money is now issued by the Federal Reserve, not the Federal government of the United States! PROOF of this is easily seen by taking a look at the face of the so-called "dollar bill". At the very top you will see the words "Federal Reserve Note", which means that piece of paper belongs to The Federal Reserve (the "big eight" families and private corporations). Hence a dollar bill is also known as a "Federal Reserve Note" or FRN for short. Sure there are other items printed on the paper to make it look "official" and to deter counterfeiting, but they mean nothing.

It was mentioned earlier that money in the U. S. used to be backed by gold and silver bullion, but the Federal Reserve has since taken away that backing. The currency system in this country is backed by nothing! It is a very rare thing to find a silver certificate in circulation in this country today, and should you come across one, it is more of a valuable collectors' item than anything else. If you have a silver certificate in your possession, you already know that it is worth more in value than is printed on it.

The Federal Reserve "loans" money to the United States Government at exorbitant interest rates, which accounts for the tremendous deficit we now have. The U. S. has to pay back more than it borrows from the Federal Reserve (the rich banking families). Here is how this system works:

1. The Federal Reserve decides that more money should be placed in circulation.
2. The United States Government goes along with this decision and authorizes the increase.
3. The Treasury Department is then instructed to print (in its printing facility) whatever amount was authorized.
4. The Treasury Department then SELLS these printed notes to The Federal Reserve Corporation for the actual cost incurred in printing the money-not for the amount printed on the face of the notes. The current cost of printing the note is about 1-1/2 cents per note.
5. The Federal Reserve then places these newly printed notes into circulation through their twelve Federal Reserve Banks from which all banking facilities in this country obtain their money. However, The Federal Reserve charges the face value of the notes to the United States Government as a loan with annual interest.
6. When the loan term ends, whether it has been paid by the U. S. Government or not, The Federal Reserve renews the loan at whatever their (the Federal Reserve's) current interest rate is.
7. Every FRN is a debt to the Federal Government of the U. S. and thus its taxpayers (that's you).
8. The Federal Reserve Act included language that put limits on the U. S. Government's right to print and spend these FRSs.
9. When the U. S. Government needs money, it borrows FRN's at the FACE VALUE from the banks (under the control of the Federal Reserve).

*WHAT YOU SHOULD KNOW BEFORE YOU COMMIT
TO DATING, MARRYING, OR STARTING A FAMILY*

10. Thus, the U. S. Government owes TWICE for every FRN placed into circulation-plus interest! As with most loans, the interest is a FIRST PRIORITY payment to the "big eight" families that own the Federal Reserve. With this kind of lending and payback system, it is easy to see that the U. S. Government can NEVER payoff its debt, no matter what any politician tells you. Want a tax refund go here http://www.uncleclayton.com/ tell uncle Clayton, zadock 1936 sent you

Chapter 14
Other Monetary Facts

Let's face it, under financing and or improper handling of money has been the destructive force of many a relationship, marriage, home or business. Just what is money? Money is a medium of exchanges for goods and/or services. How is money created? Bankers create money with just the stroke of a pen, you sign the note, and money begins coming in—your money. The banker then sells your note, creating money from your signature. Sure he has lent or is loaning you the money, but once he sells your note, the fact is your note should be marked paid in full. Instead, you keep paying the note while the banker benefits from the sale of it.

Inflation is the chief enemy of all working class people. What is inflation? Inflation is a legal means of stealing people's wealth. An example is gasoline, and every item associated with its production has been rising. Has your salary kept pace with inflation? Noooooooo. Every time you buy a product you notice the price has gone up, but your salary hasn't. This is a way the

WHAT YOU SHOULD KNOW BEFORE YOU COMMIT TO DATING, MARRYING, OR STARTING A FAMILY

system uses to keep people poor. In other words, inflation is the excessive pricing above the true value of a product—GREED.

Here is how inflation has affected your money over the years. In 2006 you paid $13.50 for what $1.00 purchased in 1941. If you earn $30,000 today, five years from today you will need to earn $50,000 just to maintain a $30,000 lifestyle. You have these facts. It's the financial future of you and your family we're speaking of, so what are you going to do about it? The wise purchase of gold and silver could be your answer. Here's why in 1975 a new Cadillac cost $8,000. You could also buy it for 230 ounces of gold. Today that same 230 ounces of one-ounce gold eagle coins will purchase three new Cadillacs and leave you $33,000 in change. Gold holds its value and protects you from inflation.

Want proof? As of today (2-17-09), click here http://www.monex.com/prods/index.html you'll see that gold eagle coins are selling for $970. an ounce, $970. x 230 ounces = $223,100. Let's say you can get a beautiful new Cadillac today for $50,000 x 3 = $150,000, leaving you $73,100. Now are you a believer in gold?

How can you achieve this gold? Hopefully these verbal affirmations as a belief system can get you there. You must keep in mind this FACT. You must develop a positive attitude and proper focus in order to bring financial freedom into your life. Reading the attitudes of wealth aloud with conviction every day is very important, because it helps to focus your mind on improving your financial future. What you focus on will manifest. What you nurture will bear fruit, so start nurturing your money tree.

1. I create my life. I create the exact amount of my financial success.
2. I play the game to win. My intention is to create wealth and abundance.
3. I admire and model rich and successful people.
4. I believe money is important, money is freedom, and money makes life more enjoyable.
5. I get rich doing what I love.
6. I deserve to be rich because I add value to other people's lives.
7. I am a generous giver and excellent receiver.
8. I am truly grateful for all the money I have now.
9. Lucrative opportunities always come my way.
10. I am incredibly blessed when it comes to money.
11. I am an excellent money manager.
12. I always pay myself first.
13. I put money into my financial freedom fund every day.
14. My money works hard for me and makes me more money.
15. I earn enough passive income to pay for my desired lifestyle.
16. I am financially free. I work because I choose to, not because I have to.
17. My part time (or full time) business is managing and investing my money, and creating passive income streams.

Chapter 15
Don't Depend on the Government

Bonus Chapter for My Fellow Readers and Associates

My name is C. L. Ray Jr. As most of you may know, I am a writer; an internationally recognized McGraw-Hill and Publish America author. They are two of the largest publishing companies in America. To verify this statement, you may Google the name above. You will find that my writings, which are part of my life's mission (to add value to other peoples lives), is being accomplished every day in the lives of many individuals on an international basis. The critical financial time in our global economy is the reason for this chapter. With all of our money (the taxpayers' money) being used to bail out those who constantly steal and or misuse the tax payer's money, I would be remiss and naive if I did not share with you a most positive way for us (the taxpayers) to create our own bail out.

I have also been active on the internet in many successful home-based business programs since the year 2000. Enough said about me. I can't add financial value and abundance to your life talking about me. Now I began the information which I hope will add value to your life as a person; it is up to you to apply it in truth to all that you do. First of all, it is my belief that all of us working programs for profit on the internet aspire to achieve financial abundance referred to as financial freedom.

There is a fact about abundance. Whether it be financial or otherwise,. it is everywhere. Just look around. It is apparent everywhere you look. Everything that God created, he did so in lavishing abundance. You can obtain and have any part you wish when you make up your mind to operate within the law. How many times have you heard someone state that we're running out of land and wonder where will they build next? Just get in your car or on an express bus and watch the abundance of land that just keeps showing up. All shortages of anything are caused by the greed and selfishness of man.

The question is, are you going about it the right way? By that I mean, are you using the sound fundamental principles and due diligence to identify what you believe to be the right opportunity for you? Have you selected that program in truth, faith, courage and commitment? And are you willing to work only that program for 12 to 18 months and see it to the apex of financial prosperity, or are you playing leap frog, jumping and leaping on every program sent your way in fear that the one program you selected might not work? Is greed letting your weak faith, courage, fear and commitment guide you into too many programs and really not arriving at the apex of financial prosperity in any of them? If this is you, read Mark 11:24.

*WHAT YOU SHOULD KNOW BEFORE YOU COMMIT
TO DATING, MARRYING, OR STARTING A FAMILY*

The above description is true for 95% of those seeking to earn money on the internet. The tragic part is, it is not totally your fault. The so called gurus send you off on a multiple income stream trip just for you to return broke and disappointed while they have grabbed your money and moved on. We all pass, or have passed, various so-called business opportunity programs around the internet. The truth is not about those programs entirely; the truth is about you. Before you attempt to sell someone else a program, have you truthfully examined it yourself?

Who are you? What is your mission in life? Is it truthfully about you helping others first (temporary self denial), or about the almighty dollar at all cost? A famous speaker once truthfully stated, "If you help enough other people get what they want, you get what you want." This is a law. It means if a fellow associate calls you for help in a program that you are not a part of and seemingly there is no benefit for you, the law is unconditional. YOU MUST still help that person. This is not easy, but it is still part of the immutable law of the universe. Also, another part of the law is whatever worthy goal it is that you wish for yourself, when you pray or dream, wish it for all who you know, don't know, love and care about, and it will return to you as sure as bread is cast upon the water.

Now, let's discuss multiple streams of income. You must first identify a program as described above and work it as stated. Then when you have a surplus, you seek diversification. How can you start four to five businesses from scratch at the same time? It is axiomatic that two things cannot occupy the same space at the same time. When you say I'm doing multiple streams of income, it is the same as saying, I think I'll start a plumbing, carpentry, nail salon, convenience store and flea market business all at the same time(except for the physical aspect). Of course there are exceptions. There are people with the money and the brain power to do this, but it is NOT THE NORM.

We all have powers, physical, mental, and spiritual; spiritual being the most powerful because it is of a higher plane. You can stay away from the hidden evils and misinformation on the internet when you use your patience, wisdom, strength, due diligence and the help of other trusted associates.

Today, I only work with a few select home based Internet programs that I have tested many times until satisfied that they will produce a steady income that I can depend on.

I continue to investigate other up and coming business opportunities that often do prove to be productive, while others prove to be not even worth my time and investment.

I also mentor new entrepreneurs, trying to place them on the right track. So many people come to me with their ideas that seem to go no where because little effort was placed into research.

I offer the reader of my book, an opportunity to contact me by email to discuss anything related to Internet Marketing. I don't usually take telephone calls unless first contacted by email. If you are interested, please use the following email address:

JABAZZ28@GMAIL.COM

IF YOU DO WRITE, PLEASE BE SURE TO TYPE THE FOLLOWING IN THE SUBJECT FIELD AT THE TOP OF THE EMAIL: "SEEKING YOUR ASSISTANCE" WHEN I SEE THOSE WORDS IN MY EMAIL BOX, I CAN RESPOND TO THEM QUICKLY.

Finally

If you can keep your head when all about you are losing theirs and blaming it on you, if and when you walk through a storm you can hold your head up high and don't be afraid of the sky, and believe at the end of the storm is a silver cloud and a golden rainbow, as you look back you will realize that you have weathered the storms of life. You wisely played the cards that life dealt you. You were able to overcome the storms of life because you never stopped reading, you never stopped growing, and you never stopped knowing that the effective implementation and direction of education is one of the best ways to add value to another person's life. To God be all the glory.

CPSIA information can be obtained at www.ICGtesting.com
Printed in the USA
BVOW081657070713

325195BV00002B/216/P